You're Going
to Be a Big
SIBLING

written by
Manon Chevallerau

odd dot

New York

illustrated by
Denise Holmes

T0006108

Dear Grown-ups,

Congratulations! Your family is about to expand, and your little one is about to take a BIG step in life—becoming a big sibling!

For parents this is also a time of big transformations, with its own concerns and excitement. Dynamics change, too. Most grown-ups wonder how to divide their love and time between multiple children, especially thinking about the elder sibling and how to keep routines and provide enough attention. Rest assured: Even during the challenging moments, a parent can draw on their love, patience, flexibility, and creativity. Your family's story is unique. You will find balance.

And I'm here to help. My name is Manon Chevallerau. As a postpartum doula and newborn expert for over two decades, I have supported thousands of families. I'm also a mom to two beautiful children, who are wonderful siblings. I wrote this book to share my expertise and to help prepare your family with safe, practical, and fun information and tools.

This book will guide you and your child through these exciting events and transform into a precious keepsake, capturing all the special moments.

With your help, my goal is to get your child ready—practically and emotionally—to become a big sibling by providing clear information and enjoyable activities.

Together, you will be creating a new family and a lifetime of love. Congratulations on all that lies ahead!

Manon

Dear Soon-to-Be Big Sibling,

Hooray! You're about to become a BIG brother or sister!

That's right. A baby—or babies if your family is expecting twins!—will soon join your family and YOU are going to be the BIG kid at home. That new baby will be your brother or sister, and together you will be siblings.

My name is Manon. I have been working with families as they welcome new babies for many years. It is such a special time when a new baby joins a family. I wanted to share my excitement by writing this book especially for you. That way, you can enjoy this time as much as I do and grow together as siblings. There's so much fun and laughter to come.

How? Well, this book will explain what you can expect and help you get ready for the baby's arrival. You will also learn how you can help when the baby arrives—and all the fun things you can do together as a new, bigger family.

Get ready to dream, draw, and sticker! This book has lots of ways you can share your feelings with your grown-ups about becoming a big sibling.

As a big sibling, you will be an important part of this new baby's life. Congratulations on all the fun that lies ahead!

3

All About Me

Draw a picture of yourself!

My name is ....

I am .... years old.

I live in ....

My family includes ....
....

My favorite

color is ....

animal is ....

food is ....

I can:

○ Dress myself

○ Use the potty

○ Read

○ Write my name

○ Put on my own shoes

My family loves to:

○ Eat meals together

○ Go to the park/
  playground together

○ Take vacations/road trips

○ Spend time with friends
  and other families

How I Found Out a New Baby Was Coming!

When did you hear the news?

Date: ....

Place: ....

Who told you about the new baby? ....

What was your reaction? ....

....

CONGRATS

YOU'RE GOING TO BE A BIG SIBLING!

Tip for Grown-ups

A wonderful way to help your child understand what it will be like when the baby is born is to visit a family with a newborn. Seeing a new baby and a new big sibling in the real world will help make the idea a concrete experience.

The doctor gave the baby's arrival a special day called the due date. When is the due date for your sibling to arrive?

Due Date:

How are you feeling about the news?

Excited   **Happy**   **Worried**   **Confused**

My family before I became a big sibling

A family is the people who love and care for you. Families come in all shapes and sizes, and every family is special. Find your favorite photo of your family now or draw what your family looks like before your little sibling arrives.

Tip for Grown-ups

Encourage your child to share this big news with a special person in their life, like a friend or grandparent. Talking about it will help them prepare for their new role as a big sibling.

What Is Pregnancy?

Have you heard a grown-up say that they are pregnant? What do you think it means? What do you notice about that person?

When a person is pregnant, a baby is growing inside of them. Growing a baby is hard work! When a grown-up is pregnant, they might need more food, water, and rest than when they are not pregnant.

How a new baby grows

Inside the pregnant person's body, in a part called the uterus, an embryo grows into a fetus. A *fetus* is the word for *baby* before it is born. During pregnancy, the fetus grows hands and feet and eyes—just like you! Then, when it's time (after about 9 months), a full-grown baby will be born.

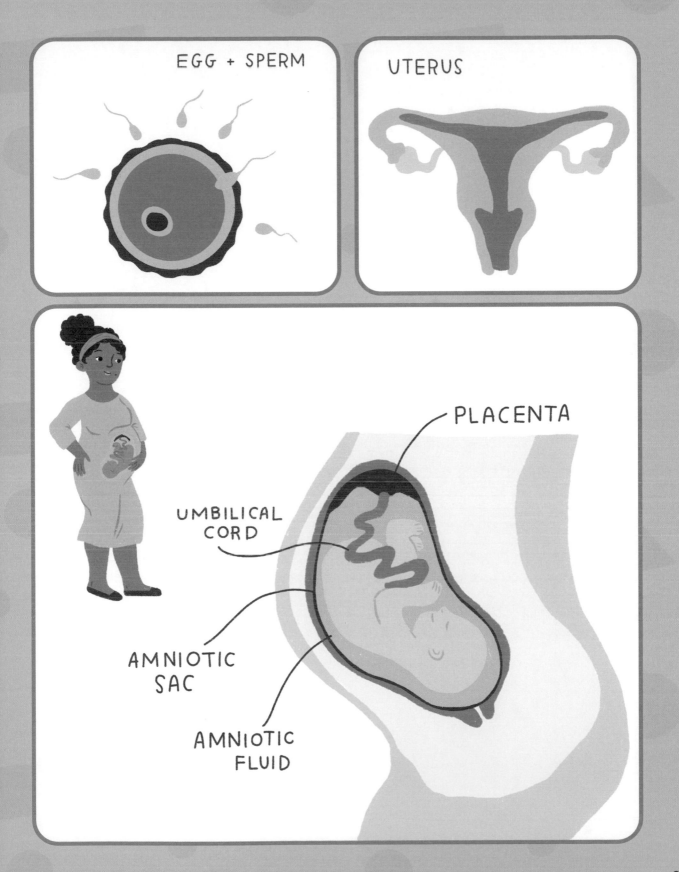

EGG + SPERM

UTERUS

PLACENTA

UMBILICAL
CORD

AMNIOTIC
SAC

AMNIOTIC
FLUID

Embryo Stages

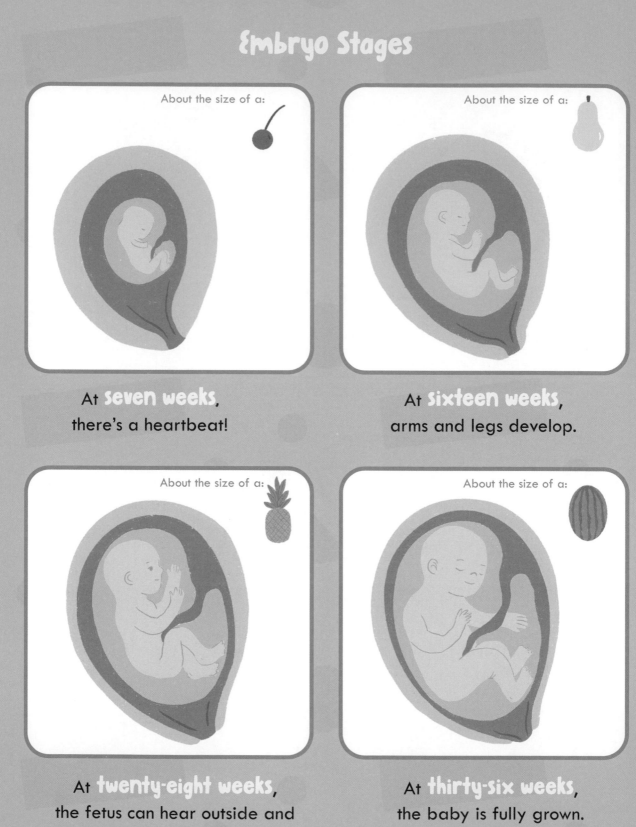

About the size of a:

At **seven weeks**,
there's a heartbeat!

About the size of a:

At **sixteen weeks**,
arms and legs develop.

About the size of a:

At **twenty-eight weeks**,
the fetus can hear outside and
see light and dark shapes.

About the size of a:

At **thirty-six weeks**,
the baby is fully grown.

Did you know . . .

The fetus feeds through a cord from their belly. Do you know what your belly button is? That's where your cord was when you were a fetus!

Feeling close

Mommy's body will keep changing and growing until the new baby is born. She might not be able to pick you up as much, but you can find other ways to cuddle with Mom. Try sitting on the couch or lying on the bed together!

Tip for Grown-ups

Now that you have shared the big news with your elder child, try to include them in the pregnancy process as much as possible. Explain to them how you are feeling, physically and emotionally. Share that there might be days that you are tired, or even feeling sick, and explain why. Help them visualize an actual small person growing inside your uterus. Print out an extra copy of the ultrasound for them to look at and save in this book.

What's in There? Your New Sibling!

Let's draw!

What does the baby look like? Draw a picture of what you think is inside Mommy's tummy. Do you want to show what the baby is hearing and seeing? What do you think the baby is doing?

Let's talk and sing with Baby!

Babies begin to hear sounds at around eighteen weeks.

Talk to the baby! They'll get to know your voice. They might even respond. Did the baby move around or kick their feet?

You can also:

PICK A SONG that you like. Get close to the belly and sing to the baby with a soft voice—not too loud!

TELL THE BABY STORIES. You can tell them about your day or tell them what you would like to do together when they are born.

Let's play with your little sibling!

Around twenty weeks, you can start feeling the baby moving in the uterus. With warm and clean hands, touch Mommy's tummy. Try staying on one spot. Does the baby react? You can also:

GUESS THE BODY PARTS! Gently touch Mommy's belly and see if you can find any bumps. What do you think they could be? Could they be the baby's head, butt, elbows, knees, or heels?

COUNT KICKS! Is the baby kicking? Count how many kicks in a minute! Does the baby kick more in the morning or evening? How do the kicks feel to you?

LISTEN TO THE HEARTBEAT!

Listen to Baby's heartbeat with a special hand-held tool called a Doppler or an electronic monitor. What does it sound like? How many beats can you count?

Tip for Grown-ups

If possible, bring your elder child to the doctor's visit so they can see the ultrasound. Ask them what the baby looks like to them!

13

Let's Prepare for Baby!

There are lots of fun ways you can get ready for the baby to arrive.

Name games

Maybe your grown-ups have a name for the baby.

Say the name when you talk to Mommy's tummy.

Write the name. Do you know all the letters?

If your grown-ups don't have a name for the baby, brainstorm one together! Write your favorite names here:

....

....

....

Tip for Grown-ups

Pick one or two routines to keep consistent with your elder child after the baby arrives. So much will change when the baby is born, and you will be very busy. It will be important for your elder child—and for you—to have some things remain the same and to spend quality time one-on-one together. Don't forget to check in with your elder child to ask how they are feeling during this transition!

Spending time together

Grown-ups will be busy taking care of the baby. Whether it's at dinnertime, bath time, story time, or playtime, make a plan for spending time together.

What are the special things you love to do with your grown-up?

Your special role in the family

Part of being a big sibling is that you get to know the baby and the baby gets to know you. You can do that by helping out with important tasks like feeding the baby and changing diapers. Make a list of things you would like to help with:

....

....

....

Tip for Grown-ups

Get your elder child a life-size baby doll to practice interacting with their new sibling. This is a great way for your elder child to build confidence and skills. They can practice holding, burping, and diapering the baby. And when the baby arrives, if they are too young to help with certain tasks, they can continue to model helping with the doll.

Baby clothes and toys

Help your grown-ups go through your old baby clothes. Look how small they are! How do you feel about sharing them with the new baby?

Go through your baby toys, too. What do you not play with anymore? Do you want to share these toys with your baby sibling? Put aside anything extra special to you.

A Place for Baby

With the baby arriving soon, there will be a special place where the baby will sleep or even a whole room for the baby called the nursery. Make a drawing to decorate the space. When you finish your artwork, ask your grown-up to help you find a nice place to display it.

Think about what you like to draw.

- Are there special things you like to look at in your room?

- Do you have favorite colors? What colors do you think the baby will like?

- What are your favorite animals? Will the baby have a stuffed animal you can draw?

- Who will be special people in the baby's life? Do you want to draw those people?

Checking in on New Experiences

So many things are happening and changing, even before the baby arrives.

How are you feeling?

You can feel a lot of things all at once. Circle all of the different feelings you are having.

HAPPY   SAD   PROUD

EXCITED   ANGRY   WORRIED

LOVE   JEALOUS   ANNOYED

Do you have questions?

Do you have any questions or worries about the pregnancy, the baby, or the birth?

Write them down here: ....

....

....

....

Tip for Grown-ups

The family is so excited leading up to the birth. For the elder sibling, this will feel abstract. They don't fully understand what is happening or exactly what is going to happen. Try to check in every week about how they are feeling. Share pregnancy milestones, let them interact with Mommy's belly, make art together, and have them talk to other kids their age about babies. Keep it light but with full awareness.

Big Sibling's Birth Plan
When will the baby arrive?

After about forty weeks or nine months of growing inside a uterus, a baby is ready to be born. No one knows the exact day the baby will be born, but grown-ups usually estimate when. They call this the due date.

What was *your* due date?

....

What day were you actually born?

....

What's the baby's due date?

....

When do you think the baby will be born? ....

How will the baby arrive?

Birth is different for everyone. Each baby arrives in their own way! The baby either comes out through a person's vagina or through the belly with the help of an operation called a C-section. The time when a baby is being born is called labor. Labor can sometimes be short (only a few hours) or long (a few days). Whether at home or at a hospital, most birthing people need a quiet and safe place to focus on getting the baby out.

When a Baby Needs Extra Care

While most babies are ready to join the family right after being born, some babies are born a little earlier than expected. These babies are called preemies and they might need to stay in the hospital for extra days or even weeks. While they are in the hospital, doctors help them to grow a little more and to breathe on their own.

... And what will Big Sibling (that's *you!*) do while Baby arrives?

Make a plan with your grown-ups to spend time with a favorite family member, grown-up friend, or nanny.

Who will you be with while the baby is arriving? ....

Write or draw what you'd like to do while you wait for your little sibling to arrive. Will you watch your favorite movie, eat your favorite foods, make special arts and crafts, or play fun games? Include the person who you will be staying with!

Here are a few fun activities to try:

DRAW A BANNER to welcome your baby sibling home! Write their name. Hang it where everyone can see it!

Think of what you will say to the baby when you meet them for the first time. You can even make up a **WELCOME SONG**!

Make a **WELCOME PRESENT** or choose one of your toys to share!

Tip for Grown-ups

Depending on your birth plan and on the age and emotional readiness of your elder child, you might want the big sibling to be present for the baby's birth. With the right preparation and planning, this can be a special way to help them understand birth and bond with the new baby. If you choose to have your elder child attend the birth, make sure that they have choices of where to be and who to be with so they can decide at any moment where they feel most comfortable.

What to Expect When Baby Comes Home

Your little sibling is almost here! Are you wondering what it will be like when they finally arrive? Here are a few things you can expect.

What will the baby be doing?
A LOT of sleeping and feeding!

In most cases, brand-new babies sleep a lot and usually wake up just to eat. They either drink breast milk from Mommy's breast, sometimes also called chest feeding, or they get a bottle with breast milk or formula. Sometimes the grown-ups and the baby will be up in the middle of the night when the baby needs to eat.

CRYING!

Since babies can't use their words, they cry to tell everyone what they need, want, or feel.

POOPING!

After the first few days, babies start to poop a lot, usually after every time they eat. The poop can be a bit watery and comes in all sorts of colors like yellow, orange, mustard, light brown, and even green.

Newborn babies can't see or hear well. They also can't hold their heads up, grab something with their hands, crawl, or walk. The baby needs the grown-ups to gently take care of them, and you can help, too.

Can you play with the baby?

Yes! You and the baby can be siblings *and* friends as you grow up. Until they grow a little bigger and can play the same way you can, you will need to keep a few things in mind when you play with the baby.

You should always have a grown-up nearby and have clean hands when you are touching, lifting, or holding the baby. Here are a few other dos and don'ts:

DON'T:

- Shake the baby

- Pull or poke the baby

- Touch the baby's eyes, nose, mouth, ears, or the soft spot on their head

- Put anything in the baby's mouth—ever!

DON'T TOUCH

SOFT SPOT

EARS

EYES

MOUTH

DO:

- Give gentle kisses on their cheeks, forehead, and hands

- Touch or pat their head, hair, cheeks, and hands

- Sing and talk to the baby in a soft voice

- Make drawings for the baby

What about Mom?

Most moms need a few weeks to rest after delivering a baby. Your mom may need extra sleep and won't be able to lift or carry you for a little while. You can still spend plenty of time together. Here are a few dos and don'ts:

TWINKLE TWINKLE ♪♫

DO:

- Give gentle cuddles in bed or on the sofa

- Read your favorite books

- Sing songs and use a quiet voice around the baby

DON'T:

- Push on Mommy's belly or breasts

- Jump on the bed or chair when the baby is feeding or is in the arms of a grown-up

- Wake Mommy or the baby when they are sleeping

Tip for Grown-ups

If the baby is born in the hospital, you can plan on the sibling's first introduction there. Depending on how you are feeling after the birth as well as the hospital regulations (make sure to check these), the big sibling can come as early as in the first hours. Planning ahead for this visit is key so there are no disappointments. Have your partner, family member, or close friend bring the sibling. Prepare them to be gentle and quiet.

Tip for Grown-ups

A wonderful way for new siblings to establish sharing and cooperation is to exchange gifts when they first meet. Have the elder sibling bring a gift they have made or picked out for the new baby. In return, have a gift from the baby ready for the elder sibling, too.

BABY IS HERE!

You've been waiting a long time, and now the baby has finally arrived. You're officially a big sibling! Write and draw some things you remember about the day that you met.

WELCOME BABY

My little sibling was born on ....

at .... at .... A.M. / P.M.

When I first met you, I felt so ....

I wanted to look at / touch / hug you.

I met you at ....

The weather was:

We named you ....

I am going to nickname you ....

I hope you and I will ....

I promise to be .... as your big sibling!

Draw your new little sibling!

Look closely at your new little sibling. Does the baby have hair? Is there a lot or little? Is it curly or straight? The baby's hands are so small—how many fingers and toes are there? Use some of your favorite crayons to draw your new little sibling.

Big and little sibling matchup!

Do you and your little sibling look alike? To investigate, find a photo of yourself when you were the same age as the baby. Paste both photos below and compare!

MY LITTLE SIBLING	ME

What else is the same or different about you and your little sibling?

BABY	ME
Birthday..................................	Birthday..................................
Length....................................	Length....................................
Weight....................................	Weight....................................
Hair color................................	Hair color................................
Eye color.................................	Eye color.................................

Hand in Hand

Sometimes your little sibling will love it when you hold their hand.

Trace one of your hands and feet with a crayon or pencil on a piece of paper. Next, choose a different colored crayon or pencil. Then, with the help of a grown-up, carefully do the same with the baby's hands and feet—making sure to place them inside your drawing.

(You can also use a copy of the baby's footprint from the hospital birth announcement.)

Now you will always be hand in hand.

It's Tummy Time!

It is important for newborns to spend some time on their tummy when they are awake during the day. It will help them become stronger.

You can start doing tummy time with your new little sibling as soon as two weeks after they are born!

Look at the moves they make. Try to copy them! Do you recognize any yoga poses?

CHILD'S POSE

SUPERMAN

PLANK

How Does It Feel to Be a Big Sibling?

Now that the baby has been born and is here to stay, let's check in on what you are thinking and feeling.

You are a big brother or sister. You may have a lot of feelings about that! Does that make you:

 Excited? If so, what are you most excited about?

....

 Happy? What makes you happy to be a big sibling?

....

 Confused? What makes you feel unsure?

....

 Worried? Are you worried when certain things happen, like when the baby cries? Any other reasons why you might be concerned? ....

Any other feelings? What do you think makes you feel that way?

....

When the baby is awake and looks at you, how does that make you feel? ....

What have you noticed about the baby?

○   The baby cries a lot

○   The baby doesn't cry a lot

○   The baby wakes up at night

○   The baby wakes me up at night

○   The baby pees and poops a lot

○   The baby needs to eat often

○   The baby doesn't eat regular food like I do

○   The baby can't hold toys yet

○   The baby can't hold their head up yet

○   The baby can't walk

     I also noticed ....

When you think about tomorrow and the day after that and the day after that, what are you most excited about as a big sibling?

○   To help the grown-ups with the baby

○   To share something special with the baby. Maybe it's your favorite story, song, or toy. Write what you want to share:

     ....

○   To play my favorite game

○   To go to the playground together

If there are moments when you feel left out, it's okay. Maybe you are getting less attention or feel a bit jealous of the baby. You might feel sad or angry AND also super happy and excited. There are a lot of changes happening around you. Try to express how you feel.

You can also make a plan to spend special time with each grown-up in your life. Maybe it is dinnertime, the bath, reading a book before bed, or going to the park.

What are some special things you would still like to do with your grown-ups?

I like to ....

    with ....

I like to ....

    with ....

I like to ....

    with ....

Tip for Grown-ups

It is very understandable and common for an elder sibling to have feelings of jealousy and confusion when they realize that the baby is not just visiting. During these moments, try to create a reset button. Spend special one-on-one time with your child. This will reinforce your special bond and reassure them of your love.

This time is a great opportunity to check in and ask what is going on in the elder sibling's life and share feelings. You can keep it light!

How to Hold a Newborn Baby

One of the first (and best) things you can do with your new baby sibling is cuddle. With the help of a grown-up, you can start by practicing first with a doll or stuffed animal. Grab your favorite plushy and follow these steps:

STEP 1: Get clean—no germs allowed!

Before you touch a baby, always wash your hands with soap and warm water, or use hand sanitizer.

STEP 2: Take a seat

Find a cozy spot to sit down. (Never hold a baby while standing up or walking around.) Place pillows around you to support your arms when they get tired. Feel comfortable and be proud—you got this!

STEP 3: Remember to support the baby's head and neck

Newborns cannot hold their heads up on their own. Babies rely on you to support their head and neck, so be sure to always support them with a hand! Remember to be very gentle.

FONTANELLE

Safety Tips for Big Siblings!

o It's your job, Big Sibling, to help keep the baby safe!

o Only hold a baby when a grown-up is present.

o Always have a grown-up hand you the baby while you are sitting down.

o Never touch the top of a baby's head. A baby has soft spots on their head called fontanelles. When touched too hard or deep it can hurt the baby.

o Do not touch the eyes, nose, mouth, or ears of the baby.

o Do not shake, poke, pull, push, or lie on top of the baby, no matter what.

STEP 4: Try the cradle hold

The cradle hold is one of the easiest and safest ways to hold a newborn for the first several weeks after they are born:

1. Now that you are clean and comfortably seated, ask a grown-up to hand the baby to you.
2. With the baby lying on their back at your chest level, slide your hand from their bottom up to support their neck.
3. Gently move the baby's head into the bend of your arm.
4. While still cradling their head, move your hand from the supporting arm to their bottom.
5. Your free arm will be able to provide extra support.

STEP 5: Check on your little sibling

Pay attention to how the baby is doing while you're holding them. If they are fussy or crying, you might try adjusting positions with a grown-up's help to see if that makes them more comfortable. You can also try a gentle and slow rocking. Baby's head should always be turned out to allow them to breathe.

YOU DID IT!
GET A STICKER

Date:

How to Bottle-feed and Burp a Baby

Time for a bottle!

The baby is hungry! Like you, the baby needs food to grow. But unlike you, the baby cannot feed themselves—they need help! And YOU can help them. Practice first with a doll or stuffed animal. You're doing great!

STEP 1: Get ready!

Sometimes babies spit up or spill milk. Have a burp cloth ready to wipe away the spit-ups or spills! Have the bottle ready, too. Don't forget to wash your hands!

STEP 2: Get into position

Who will hold the baby while they eat? If you are holding the baby, get into the holding position. Maybe a grown-up is holding the baby while you help feed them. Teamwork—that's awesome!

STEP 3: Bottle time!

Make sure that the baby's head is higher than their body. This helps them eat! Hold the bottle to their mouth carefully. Aim the nipple of the bottle at the baby's lips. You can always tickle the top of the lip with the nipple to encourage the baby to open their mouth. If they are hungry, they will latch on!

Safety Tips for Big Siblings!

- Never force the bottle into the baby's mouth.
- Be patient and be gentle!
- Don't move the baby around too much after feeding. Their tummy needs time to settle.

STEP 4: Tip the bottle

Once the baby has the bottle in their mouth, keep the bottle tipped so that the milk is at the nipple.

STEP 5: Take a break

Everyone needs to take their time when they eat! Babies need help slowing down. Take a break from feeding the baby after one ounce of milk. Count to ten, and then when everyone is ready, start again!

YOU DID IT!
GET A STICKER

Date:

Time to Burp!

While eating, babies swallow air, and that air needs to come out as a burp. Burping the baby makes your little sibling feel more comfortable. Ask a grown-up if you can help rub the baby's back while they burp. The baby might spit up!

How to Change a Baby's Diaper

Poop! Everyone does it, including your little sibling . . .
In fact, babies poop a whole lot and all the time.

Time for a fresh diaper!

STEP 1: Wash your hands

STEP 2: Get your supplies

You will need:

- a new diaper

- wipes (or if the baby is younger than six weeks old, a bowl with warm water and cotton pads)

- diaper cream

If a grown-up is changing your little sibling's diaper, you can help by bringing these things to them.

Tip for Grown-ups

A great way to help the big sibling feel more included in the care of your baby is to get a sturdy step stool. This way they can watch during diaper changes and baths, and they will feel in control when placing it where they want to be. Make sure they understand it is not okay to use it to climb into the bassinet or crib with the baby. Create other opportunities for the big sibling to participate!

STEP 3: Make the baby happy!

A grown-up will place the baby on a changing pad or table. Together, you can make sure the baby stays safely in place and calm and happy. Sing! Smile! What helps your little sibling feel happy?

STEP 4: Help change the diaper

1. Open up a new clean diaper. Hand it to a grown-up to change the baby's diaper.
2. After the grown-up has wiped and cleaned the baby's diaper area, help pat diaper cream onto the baby's skin to protect it.
3. Let a grown-up ball up the dirty diaper. You can be in charge of throwing it away!

STEP 5: Wash your hands again!

You did it! Hooray!

YOU DID IT!
GET A STICKER

Date:

39

Splish-Splash! Time for the Bath!

The first "bath"

Babies younger than two weeks old can't get their bellies totally wet. (Their umbilical cord stump has to dry up and fall off.) During this time, the baby gets a sponge bath! That is, they are wiped down with a cloth. Grown-ups may do this on the changing table with a bowl of warm water and a soft washcloth.

Bath time is fun!

Bath-time supplies

- washcloths
- the baby's towel
- a clean diaper
- clean clothes
- shampoo

Baby's first *real* bath!

Once the baby is ready, it's time for grown-ups to give the baby a real water bath. But will the baby go in your bathtub? Not yet! A grown-up will use a special, smaller, baby bathtub.

How can you help?

o Gather the bath-time supplies together with the grown-ups.
o When the grown-up puts the baby in the water, put a wet washcloth on the baby's belly to help keep the baby warm.
o Hand the grown-up the other washcloth and the shampoo.
o When the baby comes out of the tub, help gently pat the baby dry.

Your first bath-together!

When the baby is about five months old and can hold their head up and sit on their own, your grown-up may have you and the baby start taking baths together in the big tub! A grown-up will get the water temperature and level just right. Be careful not to splash too much. Show your sibling all the fun toys in your bath.

Our bath-time fun!

Draw a picture or take a photograph of sibling bath time together.

What bath-time games do you like to play together?

....

Watch the Baby Grow!

Just like you, your little sibling is growing! And each week they will learn a new way to use their body. When they start to do something special, like making eye contact or crawling, we call this a milestone.

Every baby learns these milestones at their own pace, meaning one baby might crawl or walk sooner than the other. But by the time babies are two years old, most babies catch up and can do most of the milestones below.

Keep an eye out for these milestones and don't forget to celebrate each one!

Milestones

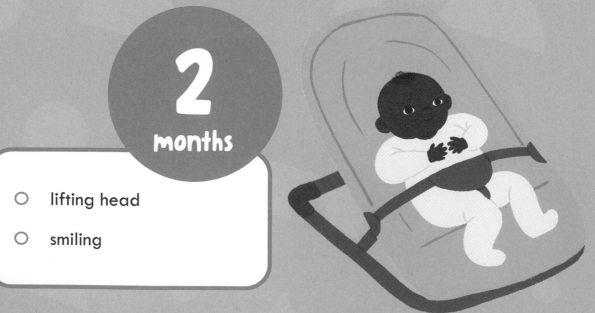

2 months

- ○ lifting head
- ○ smiling

3 months

- ○ giggling
- ○ babbling

4 months

- ○ starting to roll over
- ○ reaching for objects
- ○ holding objects

6 months

- ○ sitting
- ○ starting solid food

7 months

○ looking for hidden objects

○ dropping things on floor

9 months

○ crawling

○ pointing

○ listening to name

10 months

○ using finger and thumb

12 months

○ standing

○ walking

○ saying first words

○ waving

○ shaking objects

Let's Play!

From the very beginning, you have been your little sibling's best playmate! As your little sibling grows, you can do even more together. When the baby is about two months old, they can hear and see better and will become more aware about what is happening around them. This is a great time to try new games with the baby! Your little sibling can learn a LOT from you.

With the help of an adult, here are some activities to try with your little sibling during your first year together.

Try to get the baby to follow your lead!

STEP 1: Sit across from the baby, about an arm's length away.

STEP 2: Look the baby in the eye and make sure the baby is looking at you.

STEP 3: Slowly stick out your tongue. Pull your tongue back into your mouth. Do it again!

○ Did your little sibling follow your lead?

STEP 4: Slowly and softly say **LA LA** a few times.

○ Did your little sibling follow your lead?

STEP 5: Make an O shape and sound with your mouth.

○ Did your little sibling follow your lead?

Let's sing!

Your little sibling will love songs with hand movements. Try singing slowly and remember to use a gentle voice. Here are a few songs to start with:

"Itsy Bitsy Spider"

"If You're Happy and You Know It"

"Head, Shoulders, Knees, and Toes"

"Wheels on the Bus"

"Five Little Monkeys Jumping on the Bed"

ITSY BITSY SPIDER

Sing your favorite songs and make up hand movements to go with them, too!

Tough Times as a Big Sibling

While most of the time, you will love having a little sibling, there may also be moments that you don't want to play with your sibling or don't want to share your toys. Or maybe you simply don't want to share your grown-ups!

That is all understandable and very normal Just make sure to:

- Always use your words and not your body. Never hit, grab, pull, or bite the baby.

- If the baby grabs one of your toys, do not grab it back. Try trading with them! Hand the baby something else and then gently take back the toy and say thank you.

- Always ask for a grown-up's help when you are frustrated with the baby.

Tip for Grown-ups

Some toddlers express their frustrations and feelings with physical reactions, sometimes toward the baby, sometimes toward the grown-ups. This is normal and can happen in the beginning when the baby arrives—or weeks or even months later. Try to intervene early. Encourage the big sibling to use their words to express their feelings. Remove them from the baby or situation. Make clear that the behavior is not okay and emphasize the safety of the baby. Choose a form of discipline you have been enforcing before the baby arrived. keep an eye on the big sibling and keep communicating about feelings, sharing (things and attention from grown-ups), and use that special time together to rebuild trust.

So many ways to play together!

Laughing, dancing, exploring—there are so many things to do with your little sibling! Here are a few ideas for more games to play together. Try these or make up new games of your own!

Make funny faces and sounds for the baby.

○ Did they laugh?

Hand the baby toys.

○ Did they grab them?

Play peekaboo!

○ Did they smile?

Let's Play Outside!

With the help of an adult, here are a few fun things you can do when you are outside with your little sibling.

Match the activity stickers with your favorite ways to play!

If your little sibling is in a stroller and you are standing on a stroller step, try:

- holding hands with the baby

- singing the baby some of your favorite songs

- playing peekaboo

If you are in a calm and safe area and a grown-up is there to help you, try:

- Pushing the stroller gently—not too fast! Don't lean or push down on the stroller handlebar because the stroller might tip over.

If you are at a park or in your backyard with a grown-up, try:

- laying a blanket down and practicing tummy time together (see page 30)

- pointing out plants and animals and saying their names to the baby

If you and your grown-up are at the playground, try:

- Pushing your little sibling in a swing. Always be gentle—don't push too hard or fast!

- Going down the slide together with the help of a grown-up. Not too fast!

A Big Spoonful for Your Little Sibling

Is your little sibling six months old now? Hooray! That means they can start eating some solid foods. Since they do not have teeth yet, babies eat soft, mushy foods like purees. Over time, they'll try new foods. Around ten months, your little sibling will be able to pick up small pieces of food with their fingers!

You can help a grown-up feed your little sibling at every stage:

Eat your meals together with the baby in the high chair or booster seat.

With the help of a grown-up, feed the baby with a spoon. Babies eat with a special baby spoon that is soft and has a long handle.

Sometimes babies are fussy. You can distract the baby with a funny song so a grown-up can feed the baby.

Safety Tips for Big Siblings!

o Never give your little sibling your food. They might not be able to eat what you're eating.

o Keep a close eye on the baby! Babies can choke easily on bigger pieces of food. If you think your little sibling is choking, get a grown-up immediately.

Chef Big Sibling!

You can help prepare a puree with a grown-up. Do you like applesauce? A lot of people do—and most babies do, too!

Here's an easy recipe for applesauce with pears. Don't forget to taste-test it! Yum!

Apple & Pear Puree

You will need:

- 2 sweet apples
- 2 ripe pears
- Steamer
- Blender
- Ice cube tray

Have your grown-up help you peel and cut the apple and pear into small cubes.

STEP 1: Most foods need to be steamed since babies cannot digest solid foods easily. Steam the fruit in a saucepan with 1/2 cup (118 milliliters) of water, or in a special steamer, until soft.

STEP 2: Then, with the help of a grown-up, puree the fruits with a blender until smooth.

STEP 3: Let the fruit puree cool down and either feed it right away or save it in the freezer by using an ice cube tray for small portions.

Amazing work, chef! You made food for your baby sibling. Did you taste it?

Chef's tasting notes: Did it taste sweet? Soft? Yummy? ....

I've Been a Big Sibling for SIX Months!

Over the last few months, you have learned so much about the baby and about yourself. You are such a great big sibling! Let's look back on your time as a big sibling. How do you feel?

Are there any new things the baby can do? ....

....

Are there any new things you can do? ....

....

The baby laughs when I ....

....

The baby gets upset when ....

....

I calm the baby down by ....

....

Share some funny things you did that made the baby laugh:

....

What has changed most since the baby arrived? ....

....

What are some of your favorite things to do with your little sibling?

....

....

What do you hope you will be able to do with your little
sibling when they grow bigger? ....

....

Tape a photograph here or make a drawing of you and your little
sibling at six months.

One Year as a Big Sibling!

You did it! Your little sibling is one year old, and that means that YOU have been a big sibling for one whole year!

A first birthday is such a great milestone and such a fun thing to share with friends and family—and what better way to do that than to throw a party!

Create a special birthday card with a note for your little sibling's first birthday. What do you want to say to your little sibling on their special day? Will you include some of their favorite things?

What a day! Let's share all our favorite memories of this special moment for your family.

Where was the party? ....

Who came to celebrate? ....

Were there any games, songs, or dancing? ....

What was your favorite thing to eat at the party? ....

What was your favorite part of the party?

....

What is your special birthday wish for your little sibling? ....

Looking Back on One Year of Being a Big Sibling

Think about how much your little sibling has grown this last year. You've grown, too!

How do you feel about being a big sibling now? ....

What do you like most about being a big sibling? ....

....

What is not so great about being a big sibling? ....

....

Do you have any friends who became big siblings? ....

....

What is your favorite memory from this year? ....

....

Things you taught the baby: ....

Things that the baby taught you: ....

How you have helped out with the baby this year: ....

....

What your little sibling and you like to do together: ....

....

What's Next for Me and My Little Sibling?

Now that the baby is getting older, you do so much more together!

Here are some fun things you can look forward to doing with your sibling. Circle the ones you can't wait to do together!

- Dress up as your favorite characters or animals

- Play hide-and-seek

- Create a show for the grown-ups or friends

- Play board games

- Play tag

- Play your favorite sport

- Read books together

- Sing songs together

- Dance together

- Watch movies together

- Go camping

- Make a snowman and play in the snow

- Ride bikes together

You and Me, Forever

There's so much more ahead for you and your little sibling! Whether it's celebrations or tough times, you will always have each other. Congratulations on being a big sibling for one whole year!

BIG SIBLING ♥

CERTIFICATE OF ACHIEVEMENT

_____
NAME

_____   _____
DATE   PARENT NAME

A final note to parents

Dear Grown-ups,

If you have made it this far, you've done an awesome job nurturing your children! Bravo! The first year is always a big adjustment and achievement. Not only have you juggled a bigger family with all its commitments, but you've also found ways to empower the elder sibling. Congratulations on laying the foundation for a loving and supportive sibling relationship.

Best of luck with your beautiful family and your parenting journey!

Manon

Joyful Books for Curious Minds

An imprint of Macmillan Children's Publishing Group, LLC
Odd Dot ® is a registered trademark of Macmillan Publishing Group, LLC
120 Broadway, New York, New York 10271
OddDot.com • mackids.com

Text copyright © 2024 by Manon Chevallerau
Illustrations copyright © 2024 by Denise Holmes

All rights reserved.

DESIGNER Christina Quintero
EDITORS Nathalie Le Du and Julia Sooy

Library of Congress Cataloging-in-Publication Data is available.

ISBN 978-1-250-87481-8

Our books may be purchased in bulk for promotional, educational, or business use. Please contact your local bookseller or the Macmillan Corporate and Premium Sales Department at (800) 221-7945 ext. 5442 or by email at MacmillanSpecialMarkets@macmillan.com.

DISCLAIMER

The publisher and author disclaim responsibility for any loss, injury, or damages caused as a result of any of the instructions described in this book.

First edition, 2024

Printed in China by RR Donnelley Asia Printing Solutions Ltd., Dongguan City, Guangdong Province

10 9 8 7 6 5 4 3 2 1

Use on title page to customize your book.

Use on pages 50-51.

Brother
Sister

Super Strollers

Celebrating a first? Get a sticker!

FIRST TIME ★ BIG SIBLING ACHIEVEMENT!
HOLDING BABY

FIRST TIME ★ BIG SIBLING ACHIEVEMENT!
FEEDING BABY

FIRST TIME ★ BIG SIBLING ACHIEVEMENT!
CHANGING BABY

Playground Pals

BIG SISTER

SUPER

BIG BROTHER

YOU'RE A STAR!

YOU'RE A STAR

BIG BROTHER

BIG SISTER

BIG BROTHER

BIG SISTER